Easy Vegan Salad Dressings with NutriBullet

25 Oil Free, Plant-Based, Vegan Salad Dressing Recipes

by Sherry Inman

Copyright @2017

All rights reserved, including the right to reproduce this book or portions thereof in any form whatsoever including scanning, photocopying, or otherwise without prior written permission of the copyright holder, Sherry Inman.

Visit our website for more e-books and recipes!
freshexpresskitchen.com

The ideas and opinions expressed in this book are intended to be used for informational purposes only. Stock photos are representative, purchased through Canva. Before changing your diet, including using the plant-based, vegan recipes in this publication "Easy Vegan Salad Dressings with NutriBullet" please consult your medical professional to be sure it is appropriate for you. These recipes were created to fit into a healthy diet regimen, no individual results or health effects can be guaranteed, predicted or foreseen.

ISBN-13: 978-1544870724

ISBN-10: 1544870728

Table of Contents

Introduction……4
Helpful Tips……5
Apricot Orange Vinaigrette…..6
Asian Sesame Dressing……7
Avocado Cilantro Dressing……8
Blueberry Balsamic Vinaigrette……9
Buttermilk Dressing……10
Catalina Dressing……11
Caesar Dressing……12
Cilantro Lime Vinaigrette……13
Coconut Lime Curry Dressing……14
Creamy Italian Dressing……15
Dijon Poppy Seed Dressing……16
French Dressing……17
Garden Olive Vinaigrette……18
Greek Salad Dressing……19
Green Goddess……20
Italian Herb Dressing…….21
Lemon Thyme Vinaigrette……22
Mango Dressing……23
Maple Balsamic Dressing……24
Miso Dressing……25
Ranch Dressing……26
Roasted Red Pepper Vinaigrette……27
Strawberry Cilantro Vinaigrette……28
Thai Sweet Chili Dressing……29
Thousand Island Dressing……30
Thank you!……31

Introduction

If you're new to the high carb, low fat, vegan diet, this book is for you! Making your own homemade plant-based, vegan salad dressing is quick & easy with the NUTRiBullet! These vegan salad dressings have been artfully created with herbs, spices, and select seeds and nuts which will complement most raw salads, steamed vegetables, baked potatoes, pasta salads, and stir-fry's. They can even be used as a dip for snack trays! These dressings are nutrient-rich, low in sugar, and low in fat, so you can feel good about what you are eating!

We hope you enjoy these homemade, flavorful versions of your favorites!
~Sherry

Helpful Tips

Most dressings will keep well in the fridge in a sealed container for a week or so, thanks to the natural preservative properties of vinegar and lemon.

If your dressing thickened while it chilled, simply thin it with a little nut milk or water.

Make a double batch of your favorite dressing and use it as a marinade, a raw veggie dip, a base to make a potato or pasta salad.

Mason jars are perfect for serving and storing homemade salad dressings.

Stevia and maple syrup add a little sweetness to these recipes, feel free to use the sweetener you prefer.

Just the right amount of Sea Salt or (Pink Himalayan) and pepper is an individual preference, tweak the recipe to get it just right for you.

Apricot Orange Vinaigrette

1/4 cup 100% fruit apricot preserves

3-4 dried apricots

1 mandarin orange, peeled

2 tablespoons rice vinegar

1/8 teaspoon paprika

2 tablespoons apple cider vinegar

1 tablespoon chia seeds

3/4 cup water

pinch of sea salt & black pepper to taste

3-5 drops stevia and / or 1 - 2 teaspoons maple syrup

*Place all ingredients in the
NUTRiBullet and pulse. Refrigerate until well chilled.*

Asian Sesame Dressing

1/4 cup rice wine vinegar

1 teaspoon ginger root (or 1/2 tsp powder ginger)

1 tablespoon tamari sauce or coconut amino

3 drops sesame oil (optional)

2 tablespoons sunflower seeds

1/2 cup water

2 tablespoons sesame seeds, toasted

pinch of sea salt & black pepper to taste

3-5 drops stevia and / or 1 - 2 teaspoons maple syrup

Place all ingredients in the NUTRiBullet and pulse. Refrigerate until well chilled.

Avocado Cilantro Dressing

1 avocado, peeled with seed removed

1/4 tsp basil, dried

1/2 cucumber

1/4 teaspoon dill weed, dried

1/2 teaspoon garlic powder

2 limes, juiced

1/3 cup cashews, soaked 15 min

1 green onion

1/2 cup fresh cilantro

1/2 cup unsweetened nut milk

pinch of sea salt & black pepper to taste

3-5 drops stevia and / or 1 - 2 teaspoons maple syrup

Place all ingredients in the NUTRiBullet and pulse. Refrigerate until well chilled.

Blueberry Balsamic Vinaigrette

4 tablespoons balsamic vinegar

2 tablespoons maple syrup

1 tablespoon lemon juice

1 tablespoons chia seeds

3/4 cup water

1 cup fresh blueberries

pinch of sea salt & black pepper to taste

3-5 drops stevia and / or 1 - 2 teaspoons maple syrup

Place all ingredients in the NUTRiBullet and pulse. Refrigerate until well chilled.

Buttermilk Dressing

1 green onion

1 tablespoon lemon juice, freshly squeezed

1 tablespoon Dijon mustard

1/2 cup plain hummus

1 teaspoon paprika

1 tablespoon nutritional yeast

1/4 teaspoon garlic powder

1/3 cup cashews, soaked 15 min

1/2 cup unsweetened soy milk

1/2 cup plain vegan sour cream

1/4 teaspoon apple cider vinegar

pinch of sea salt & black pepper to taste

3-5 drops stevia and / or 1 - 2 teaspoons maple syrup

Place all ingredients in the NUTRiBullet and pulse. Refrigerate until well chilled.

Catalina Dressing

1/4 cup ketchup

1/2 cup apple cider vinegar

1/2 teaspoon onion powder

1/2 teaspoon paprika

1/3 cup cashews, soaked 15 min & drained

1/2 cup unsweetened nut milk

pinch of sea salt & black pepper to taste

3-5 drops stevia and / or 1 - 2 teaspoons maple syrup

Place all ingredients in the NUTRiBullet and pulse. Refrigerate until well chilled.

Caesar Dressing

1/4 cup plain hummus

1 teaspoon spicy mustard

1/2 teaspoon lemon zest

2-3 tablespoons lemon juice, to taste

2 teaspoon capers

3 teaspoon brining juice

4-5 cloves fresh garlic

pinch of sea salt & black pepper to taste

3-5 drops stevia

Place all ingredients in the NUTRiBullet and pulse. Refrigerate until well chilled.

Cilantro Lime Vinaigrette

1/2 teaspoon garlic powder

1/4 cup cilantro

1 tsp Dijon mustard

1/4 cup lime juice, fresh

1 tablespoon chia seeds

3/4 cup unsweetened nut milk

1/4 teaspoon cumin

pinch of sea salt & black pepper to taste

3-5 drops stevia and / or 1 - 2 teaspoons maple syrup

Place all ingredients in the NUTRiBullet and pulse. Refrigerate until well chilled.

Coconut Lime Curry Dressing

1 can coconut milk

1/4 cup creamy peanut butter

1 tablespoon Thai curry paste

1 clove garlic

juice of a lime

1-2 teaspoons Sriracha

1 tablespoon apple cider vinegar

1 teaspoon turmeric

1/4 cup chopped fresh basil

pinch of sea salt & black pepper to taste

3-5 drops stevia and / or 1 - 2 teaspoons maple syrup

Place all ingredients in the NUTRiBullet and pulse. Refrigerate until well chilled.

Creamy Italian Dressing

2/3 cup unsweetened nut milk

1/2 cup raw cashews, soaked 15 min

1/3 cup lemon juice

1/2 teaspoon garlic powder or 1 clove garlic

2 teaspoon dried parsley

2 teaspoon dried basil

1 teaspoon dried oregano

1/4 yellow onion

1/2 cup plain vegan yogurt

pinch of sea salt & black pepper to taste

3-5 drops stevia and / or 1 - 2 teaspoons maple syrup

Place all ingredients in the NUTRiBullet and pulse. Refrigerate until well chilled.

Dijon Poppy Seed Dressing

1/2 cup plain vegan yogurt

1/3 cup apple cider vinegar

1/4 yellow onion

1 teaspoon Dijon mustard

1/3 cup cashews, soaked 15 min

1 tablespoon poppy seed

pinch of sea salt & black pepper to taste

3-5 drops stevia and / or 1 - 2 teaspoons maple syrup

Place all ingredients in the NUTRiBullet and pulse. Refrigerate until well chilled.

French Dressing

1/3 cup ketchup (low sugar)

2 tablespoons sunflower seeds

1/2 cup water

1/4 cup white vinegar

1/4 lemon, peel removed

1/4 teaspoon paprika

1/4 cup plain vegan yogurt

1 clove garlic

1/2 - 1 small shallot

pinch of sea salt & black pepper to taste

3-5 drops stevia and / or 1 - 2 teaspoons maple syrup

Place all ingredients in the NUTRiBullet and pulse until creamy. Refrigerate until well chilled.

Garden Olive Vinaigrette

1/3 cup white wine vinegar

2 tablespoons chia

1 cup water

2 cloves garlic

1 tablespoon Italian seasoning

1/4 teaspoon red pepper flakes

1 tablespoon Dijon mustard

1/2 cup plain vegan yogurt

1/2 apple

1 yellow mini pepper or 1/4 yellow bell pepper

pinch of sea salt & black pepper to taste

3-5 drops stevia and / or 1 - 2 teaspoons maple syrup

Place all ingredients in the NUTRiBullet and pulse until smooth. Refrigerate until well chilled.

Greek Salad Dressing

2 - 3 Greek black olives, pitted

1 pepperoncini

2 tablespoons sunflower seeds

1/2 cup water

1/3 cup white wine vinegar

1 tablespoon Dijon mustard

1 tablespoon apple cider vinegar

1 clove fresh garlic

1 small shallot

1 tablespoon dried Italian seasoning

1/2 teaspoon dried thyme

1/2 teaspoon dried rosemary

pinch of sea salt & black pepper to taste

3-5 drops stevia and / or 1 - 2 teaspoons maple syrup

Place all ingredients in the NUTRiBullet except Italian seasoning and pulse until creamy smooth. Add Italian seasoning, give it a whisk, and refrigerate until chilled.

Green Goddess

1/3 cup cashews, soaked and drained

1 tablespoon chopped parsley

1/2 cup chopped green onion

1 tablespoon sesame seeds

2 tablespoon tamari sauce or coconut amino

2 tablespoons apple cider vinegar

2 tablespoons lemon juice

2 garlic cloves

1/2 cup coconut milk or almond milk

pinch of sea salt & black pepper to taste

2-4 drops stevia to taste and / or 1 - 2 teaspoons maple syrup

Place all ingredients in the NUTRiBullet except and pulse until creamy smooth. Refrigerate until well chilled.

Italian Herb Dressing

2 green olives, pitted

1 tablespoons chia seeds

3/4 cup of water

1/2 cup white wine vinegar

1 tablespoon grated Vegan Parmesan

1 garlic clove

1 teaspoon dried oregano

pinch of sea salt & black pepper to taste

3-5 drops stevia and / or 1 - 2 teaspoons maple syrup

Place all ingredients in the NUTRiBullet except oregano seasoning and pulse until creamy smooth. Add oregano seasoning, give it a good whisk or stir, and refrigerate until well chilled.

Lemon Thyme Vinaigrette

1/4 cup lemon juice

1/4 cup apple cider vinegar

2 tablespoons chia seeds

1 cup water

1/2 cup plain vegan yogurt

1 tablespoon thyme

1 teaspoon Dijon mustard

1 teaspoon poppy seeds

pinch of sea salt & black pepper to taste

3-5 drops stevia and / or 1 - 2 teaspoons maple syrup

Place all ingredients in the NUTRiBullet, except poppy seeds, and pulse until smooth. Add poppy seeds, give it a good whisk or stir, and refrigerate until well chilled.

Mango Dressing

1 whole mango peeled
1/4 cup apple cider vinegar
1/4 cup orange juice
2 tablespoons fresh lime juice
1 teaspoon Dijon mustard
1/4 cup cashews, soaked 15 min & drained
1/2 cup water
1/2 teaspoon grated lime zest
pinch of sea salt
3-5 drops stevia and / or 1 - 2 teaspoons maple syrup

Place all ingredients (except lime zest) in the NUTRiBullet and pulse until smooth. Whisk in lime zest. Refrigerate until well chilled.

Maple Balsamic Dressing

1/3 cup balsamic vinegar

2 tablespoons coarse-grained mustard

1/3 cup maple syrup

2 tablespoons chia seeds

1 cup water

pinch of sea salt & black pepper to taste

Place all ingredients in the NUTRiBullet and pulse until smooth. Refrigerate until well chilled.

Miso Dressing

2 tablespoons apple cider vinegar

1/4 cup nutritional yeast

2 tablespoons sunflower seeds

1/2 cup water

2 teaspoons yellow mustard

1 teaspoon brown mustard

3 teaspoons miso

pinch of sea salt & black pepper to taste

3-5 drops stevia and / or 1 - 2 teaspoons maple syrup

Place all ingredients in the NUTRiBullet and pulse until smooth. Refrigerate until well chilled.

Ranch Dressing

1/3 cup cashews, soaked 15 minutes & drained

1/2 cup unsweetened nut milk

2 teaspoons apple cider vinegar

2 fresh chives, minced fine

2 fresh chives, whole

1 teaspoon dried dill

2 teaspoons dried parsley

2 teaspoons onion powder

1 teaspoon garlic powder

pinch of sea salt & black pepper to taste

3-5 drops stevia and / or 1 - 2 teaspoons maple syrup

Place all ingredients in the NUTRiBullet (except minced chives and dill) and pulse until smooth. Whisk in minced chives and dill. Refrigerate until well chilled.

Roasted Red Pepper Vinaigrette

1/3 cup cashews, soaked and drained

1/2 cup water

2 red bell peppers, roasted & peeled

1 shallot

1/3 cup white balsamic vinegar

2 tablespoons Dijon mustard

pinch of sea salt & black pepper to taste

3-5 drops stevia and / or 1 - 2 teaspoons maple syrup

Place all ingredients in the NUTRiBullet and pulse until smooth. Refrigerate until well chilled.

Strawberry Cilantro Vinaigrette

1 cup fresh strawberries

2 tablespoons chia seeds

1 cup water

1/4 cup balsamic vinegar

1/2 cup cilantro leaves, minced

1 tablespoon Dijon mustard

pinch of sea salt & black pepper to taste

3-5 drops stevia and / or 1 - 2 teaspoons maple syrup

Place all ingredients in the NUTRiBullet (except cilantro) and pulse until smooth. Add cilantro and whisk together. Refrigerate until well chilled.

Thai Sweet Chili Dressing

1 tsp Sriracha hot chili sauce

2 cloves garlic

1/2 teaspoon red pepper flakes

2 tablespoons tamari sauce

2 tablespoons rice vinegar

1 tablespoon fresh lime juice

1/2 teaspoon miso

1/4 cup peanut butter

2 tablespoons chia seeds

1 cup water

pinch of sea salt & black pepper to taste

3-5 drops stevia and / or 1 - 2 teaspoons maple syrup

Place all ingredients in the NUTRiBullet and pulse until smooth. Refrigerate until well chilled.

Thousand Island Dressing

3 tablespoons sunflower seeds

1/2 cup sun-dried tomatoes, rehydrate and drained

1 cup water

5 tablespoon lemon juice

1 tsp onion powder

1/2 tsp garlic powder

2 tablespoons raw apple cider vinegar

1/2 cup red onions, finely chopped

1/2 cup sweet pickle, minced

pinch of sea salt & black pepper to taste

3-5 drops stevia and / or 1 - 2 teaspoons maple syrup

Combine all ingredients (except red onion & sweet pickle) in the NUTRiBullet and pulse. Stir in the onions and pickle. Refrigerate until well chilled.

Thank you!

Other vegan books:
Kale Yeah! Detox and Look Radiant!
20 Easy Juice Recipes with Healing Herbs

Subscribe to our "Amazon Author Page" for new releases!

www.amazon.com/author/sherryinman

Please visit our online Vegan Recipe Collection!

www.Freshexpresskitchen.com

Made in the USA
Las Vegas, NV
07 November 2023

80425121R00019